WHEN A PARENT GOES TO JAIL

A Comprehensive Guide for Counseling Children of Incarcerated Parents

written by

Rebecca M. Yaffe and Lonnie F. Hoade

illustrated by

Barbara S. Moody

Rayve Productions Inc.

Rayve Productions Inc.
Box 726 Windsor CA 95492

Printed in China

Illustrated by Barbara S. Moody

Library of Congress Cataloging-in-Publication Data

When a Parent Goes to Jail : a comprehensive guide for counseling children of incarcerated parents / written by Rebecca M. Yaffe and Lonnie F. Hoade ; illustrated by Barbara S. Moody.
    p. cm.
    Includes glossary
    Summary: Explains rules, laws, choices, and consequences resulting in going to jail, discusses what to expect from the legal system, and provides advice on coping with having a parent in jail.
    ISBN 1-877810-08-8 (alk. paper)
    1. Children of prisoners--Counseling of--Juvenile literature. 2. Children of prisoners--Services for--Juvenile literature. 3. Imprisonment--Juvenile literature. 4. Child psychology--Juvenile literature. [1. Prisoners. 2. Prisons.] I. Hoade, Lonnie F., 1954- II. Moody, Barbara S., ill. III. Title.

HV8885 .Y33 2000
362.7--dc21
                                                                                                       99-087379

To the
Warren Counseling Center
Lynchburg College
Lynchburg, Virginia

Contents

Glossary

arrest:	When a person is captured by the police and held for a period of time.
cell:	Small, locked room, sometimes with bars.
chaotic:	When things are in total disorder or confusion.
cope:	To handle and deal with a feeling or situation successfully.
confused:	When you are unclear about what is going on.
court:	A room or building in which a judge listens and decides if a law has been broken.
consequences:	Something that happens when you don't follow rules or laws.
embarrassed:	When you feel nervous or have an uncomfortable feeling about something.
guard:	An adult in uniform who watches over prisoners to make sure that they do not escape.
guilty:	When someone is at fault or responsible for something that happened.
judge:	An adult who listens and makes decisions in a court of law.
possessions:	Things that people own.
punishment:	A penalty or consequence for doing something wrong.
released:	When someone is set free or let go from jail.
visitation:	When you go to see your parent in jail.

Rules, Laws and Consequences

The world is a big place with lots of people who have to live and work together, so we need rules. There are rules at home, at school, and even on the bus. In fact, there are rules for almost everything we do.

Rules are made for lots of reasons. We have rules for fairness, rules to keep us safe, rules to teach us how to act, and rules to keep things running smoothly. Without rules, the world would be a chaotic and dangerous place.

Everyone chooses to break the rules sometimes. But when rules are broken there are consequences. If you break a rule you might be sent to time out or lose your recess or have to talk to the principal. Sometimes you might have to stay in your room away from your friends and family. These are the consequences of choosing to break the rules. Consequences help you learn to make better choices.

There are special rules called laws. Laws are made to keep people and their possessions safe. When people choose to break the law, there are consequences, too. Going to jail is one consequence of breaking the law.

Why a Parent Is Arrested

When a parent chooses to break the law, there are consequences.

Some parents are given tickets when they break a law like speeding or parking in the wrong place.

Other parents have to be arrested and spend time in jail
when they break a big law, like drinking and driving,
or stealing, or using drugs.

The Arrest

Sometimes the police arrest a parent when
he or she is at work.

You don't see the arrest because you are at home,

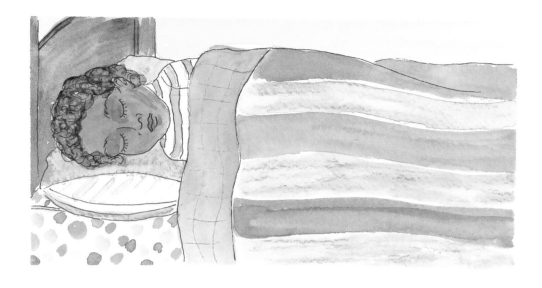

or in school.

Other times, the police may come to your house to arrest your parent. You see the police handcuff your parent.

and drive him or her away in a police car.

Where the Police Officers
Take Your Parent

The police officers take your parent to a jail where
they take a picture of him or her.

and
fingerprint them.

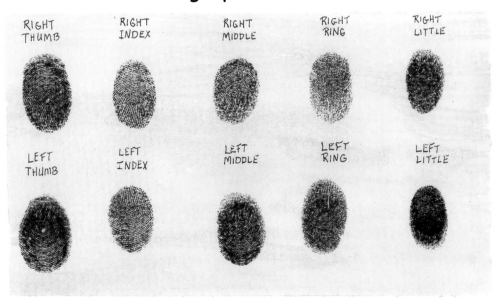

Your parent is then placed in a locked cell until he or she goes to court.

In court a judge or jury decides if your parent is guilty of breaking the law. The judge decides how long your parent should stay in jail.

Then your parent is taken to a bigger jail, sometimes called a prison. This is where your parent stays until the court says he or she can come home.

Going to jail helps some parents learn to make better choices and stop breaking the law.

What Are You Feeling?

When your parent goes to jail it is only natural that you will have many different feelings.

Sad

Scared

Angry

Confused

Worried

Embarrassed

Safe and Relieved

Unloved by the parent in jail

There are things you can do to understand your feelings
better. And understanding your feelings will help you handle
(cope with) them until your parent comes home.

What would happen if you didn't share your feelings?
They'd keep building up inside you.

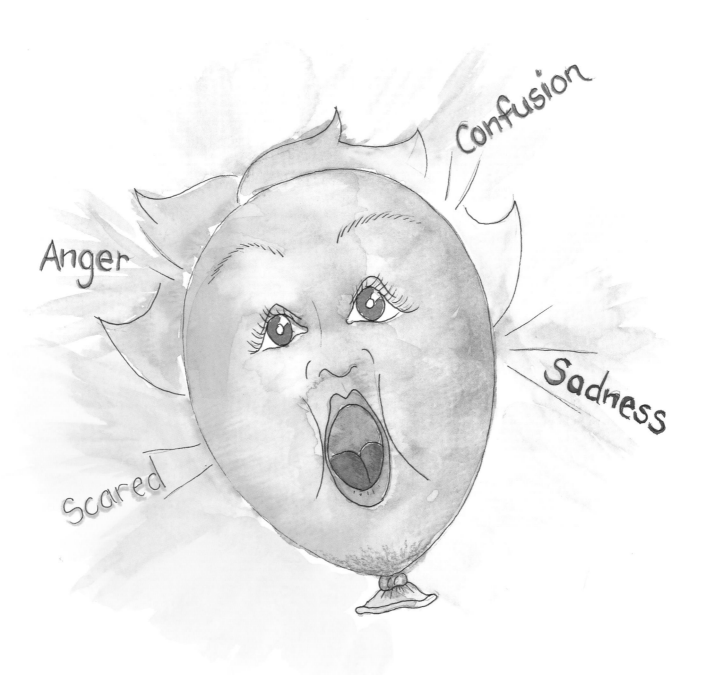

It helps to talk to someone about your feelings.
You can talk to your other parent

or to a relative.

It may help to talk to a counselor. Usually, there is a school counselor available for you to talk to,

Or you might meet with a counselor in an office.

Very often, it helps to share your feelings with a group of children who also have a parent in jail. They know how you feel because they have been through it, too.

Feelings and Thoughts About the Parent in Jail

Sometimes you may feel like you hate your parent who is in jail. It's okay to hate what your parent did and even be mad at him or her for doing it.
But hating your parent will hurt both of you.

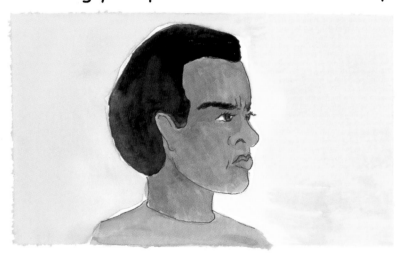

People say that a person who goes to jail is bad. You may wonder if your parent is a bad person now. Your parent is not a bad person. He or she made a bad choice and did a bad thing.

It's okay to still love your mom or dad and show that you do.

Changes at Home

When one parent is in jail, it almost always means there will be changes at home. Your other parent may have less time to spend doing fun things with you.

Your family may not have as much money, so you may not be
able to have or do as many things as you did
before your parent went to jail.

You could have to help out more by doing extra chores.

Changes at School

It may be difficult to go to school. When others ask about your parent in jail, you might feel uncomfortable or embarrassed. You might be worried that your friends won't like you anymore.

Try to remember, you haven't changed, even if your parent is in jail. Real friends will stand by you and be there when you need someone to talk to.

Visitation

After a while you may be able to visit your parent in jail. You might have mixed feelings about visiting him or her the first time. It's normal to feel excited about seeing your parent.

but,
you might also feel scared about visiting the jail,

or,
you may not want to visit your parent in jail at all. It is
important to discuss these feelings with your parent.

When you first visit the jail, guards search you and your family before you go inside. This is to protect you and your family as well as the other people in jail.

There are lots of different jails and all have their own rules about visitation. In some jails, you have to see your parent through a glass panel and talk to him or her on a telephone.

In other jails, you can visit with your parent in a big room with other prisoners and their families.

Sometimes you and your family get to visit your parent outside in a big yard.

Visiting your parent can help both of you feel better. It helps to see your parent and know that he or she is okay. It will help your parent to see you and know that you are okay, too.

When you can't visit the jail, you can write letters to one another. It helps to send pictures with your letters.

Sometimes your parent is allowed to call you from jail. It helps to hear each other's voice when you are separated.

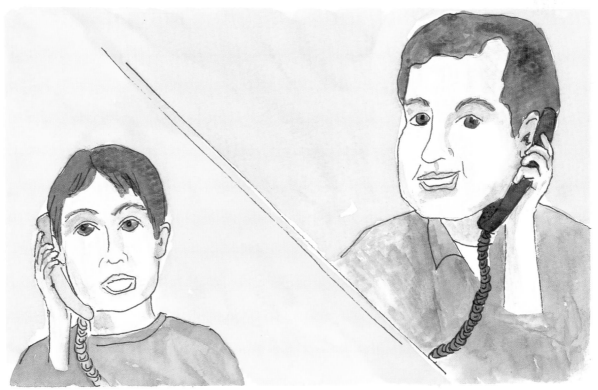

Your Parent Comes Home

One day your parent may get released from jail and return home. Each person in the family will have lots of different feelings about your parent's return. Some might be happy. Some might be shy. Some might be nervous. And some might even have all these feelings and more.

At first, you may feel like you have a guest staying with you,
the same way you feel when your grandparents
or aunts and uncles come to visit.

It takes time to adjust to the changes in your home when your father or mother returns from jail. Your parent may want to share in your daily activities. He or she may want to help you with homework, or take you to a movie, or read a story to you before bed. These are things you are used to doing with your other parent. It's okay to share this time.

There were lots of changes when your parent left, and there will be lots more when he or she comes home. It is normal to like things to stay the same, but, sometimes, change can be good. Going to jail, like any punishment, helps some parents learn to make better choices and stop breaking laws.

CHILDREN'S BOOKS & MUSIC

☆ *Buffalo Jones: The man who saved America's bison*

by Carol A. Winn; illustrated by William J. Geer

ISBN 1-877810-30-4, hardcover, $12.95, 2000 pub.

In this true story, Charles Jesse "Buffalo" Jones undertakes a treacherous 1800s Texas trail ride, risking his life to rescue baby buffalo and save America's bison from extinction. The Old West comes alive in this exciting and humorous adventure that boys and girls are sure to enjoy. Includes a glossary and dozens of lively black and white illustrations. (Ages 10-14)

☆ *Link Across America: A story of the historic Lincoln Highway*

by Mary Elizabeth Anderson

ISBN 1-877810-97-5, hardcover, $14.95, 1997 pub.

It began with a long-ago dream . . . a road that would run clear across America! The dream became reality in 1914 as the Lincoln Highway began to take form, to eventually run from New York City to San Francisco. Venture from past to present experiencing transportation history. Topics include Abraham Lincoln, teams of horses, seedling miles, small towns, making concrete, auto courts, Burma Shave signs, classic cars and road rallies. Color photos along today's Lincoln Highway remnants, black and white historical photos, map and list of cities along the old Lincoln Highway. (Ages 6-13)

☆ *The Perfect Orange: A tale from Ethiopia*

by Frank P. Araujo, Ph.D.; illustrated by Xiao Jun Li

ISBN 1-877810-94-0, hardcover, $16.95, 1994 pub., Toucan Tales volume 2

Inspiring gentle folktale. Breathtaking watercolors dramatize ancient Ethiopia's contrasting pastoral charm and majesty. Illustrations are rich with Ethiopian details. Story reinforces values of generosity and selflessness over greed and self-centeredness. Glossary of Ethiopian terms and pronunciation key. (Ages 4-13)
(**PBS** *Storytime* **Selection**; Recommended by *School Library Journal, Faces, MultiCultural Review, Small Press Magazine, The Five Owls, Wilson Library Bulletin*)

☆ *Nekane, the Lamiña & the Bear: A tale of the Basque Pyrenees*

by Frank P. Araujo, Ph.D.; illustrated by Xiao Jun Li

ISBN 1-877810-01-0, hardcover, $16.95, 1993 pub., Toucan Tales volume 1

Delightful Basque folktale pits appealing, quick-witted young heroine against mysterious villain. Lively, imaginative narrative, sprinkled with Basque phrases. Vibrant watercolor images. Glossary of Basque terms and pronunciation key. (Ages 6-10)
(Recommended by *School Library Journal, Publishers Weekly, Kirkus Reviews, Booklist, Wilson Library Bulletin, The Basque Studies Program Newsletter: University of Nevada, BCCB, The Five Owls*)

☆ *The Laughing River: A folktale for peace*

by Elizabeth Haze Vega; illustrated by Ashley Smith, 1995 pub.

ISBN 1-877810-35-5 **hardcover book**, $16.95, ISBN 1-877810-36-3 **companion musical audiotape**, $9.95; ISBN 1-877810-37-1 **book & musical audiotape combo**, $23.95,; **Drum kit**, $9.95,; **Book, musical audiotape & drum kit combo**, $29.95,

Two fanciful African tribes are in conflict until the laughing river bubbles melodiously into their lives, bringing fun, friendship, peace. Lyrical fanciful folktale of conflict resolution. Mesmerizing music. Dancing, singing and drumming instructions. Orff approach. (Ages 5-12) (Recommended by *School Library Journal)*

☆ *When Molly Was in the Hospital: A book for brothers and sisters of hospitalized children*

by Debbie Duncan; illustrated by Nina Ollikainen, M.D.

ISBN 1-877810-44-4, hardcover, $12.95, 1994 pub.

Anna's little sister, Molly, has been very ill and had to have an operation. Anna tells us all about the experience from her point of view. Sensitive, insightful, heartwarming story. A support and comfort for siblings and those who love them. Authentic. Realistic. Effective. (Ages 3-12)
(**Winner of 1995 Benjamin Franklin Award: Best Children's Picture Book.** Recommended by *Children's Book Insider, School Library Journal, Disabilities Resources Monthly*)

☆ *Night Sounds*

by Lois G. Grambling; illustrated by Randall F. Ray

ISBN 1-877810-77-0, hardcover, $12.95   ISBN 1-877810-83-5, softcover, $6.95, 1996 pub.

Perfect bedtime story and a great beginning reader. Ever so gently, a child's thoughts slip farther and farther away, moving from purring cat at bedside and comical creatures in the yard to distant trains and church bells, and then at last, to sleep. Imaginative, lilting text and daringly unpretentious black and white illustrations. (Ages 4-6)

☆ *Los Sonidos de la Noche*

by Lois G. Grambling; illustrated by Randall F. Ray

(Spanish edition of *Night Sounds*), 1996 pub.

ISBN 1-877810-76-2, hardcover, $12.95   ISBN 1-877810-82-7, softcover, $6.95

☆ *Nicky Jones and the Roaring Rhinos*

by Lois G. Grambling; illustrated by William J. Geer

ISBN 1-877810-14-2, hardcover, $13.95, 2000 pub.

With the help of four big brothers, Nicky Jones learns to play football, becomes a spectacular player, and surprises teammates at story's end. Award-winning author Lois Grambling has written a delightful book, and her easy-to-read style and the lively, colorful illustrations will keep young readers chuckling and turning pages. (Ages 6-8).

PARENTING

☆ *Joy of Reading: One family's fun-filled guide to reading success*

by Debbie Duncan

ISBN 1-877810-45-2, softcover, $14.95, 1998 pub.

A dynamic author and mother, and an expert on children's literature, shares her family's personal reading success stories. You'll be inspired and entertained by this lighthearted, candid glimpse into one family's daily experiences as they cope with the ups and downs of life. Through it all, there is love, and an abundance of wonderful books to mark the milestones along the way.

"*Joy of Reading* is the perfect guide to great children's books . . . the perfect foundation reference for parents wanting to instill a love of reading and literature in their children. Ideal for developing home-schooling reading curriculums as well."

— The Midwest Book Review

COUNSELING

☆ *When a Parent Goes to Jail: A comprehensive guide for counseling children of incarcerated parents*

by Rebecca M. Yaffe and Lonnie F. Hoade

ISBN 1-877810-08-8, hardcover, $49.95, 2000 pub.

Professional counselors help children understand rules, laws, choices and consequences, why their parents are in jail, what to expect in the legal system and how to cope with their emotions. (Ages 5-12)

☆ *When a Parent Goes to Jail Workbook*

by Rebecca M. Yaffe and Lonnie F. Hoade

ISBN 1-877810-11-8, softcover, $29.95, 2000 pub.

This professionally developed companion workbook to the above guide contains writing and drawing activities that help children develop understanding and work through complex emotions. (Ages 5-12)

HISTORY

☆ *20 Tales of California: A rare collection of western stories*

by Hector Lee

ISBN 1-877810-62-2, softcover, $9.95, 1998 pub.

Masterfully written stories filled with drama, adventure, intrigue and humor. Mysterious and romantic, real life and folklore set in various California locations. Drawn from the folklore and local history of California, most of the stories are about real people. They are essentially true, based on historical facts, but some are folklore, too, as folk remembered the truth or have fashioned it into local legend. Includes ideas for family outings and classroom field trips and discussion questions. (Ages 14-adult)

☆ *Buffalo Jones: The man who saved America's bison* — see Children's Books

☆ *Link Across America: A story of the historic Lincoln Highway* — see Children's Books

ORDER

For mail orders please complete this order form and forward with check, money order or credit card information to Rayve Productions, POB 726, Windsor CA 95492. If paying with a credit card, you can call us toll-free at 800.852.4890 or fax this completed form to Rayve Productions at 707.838.2220.

You can also order at our Web site at www.spannet.org/rayve.

☐ Please send me the following book(s):

Title _____	Price _____	Qty _____	Amount _____
Title _____	Price _____	Qty _____	Amount _____
Title _____	Price _____	Qty _____	Amount _____
Title _____	Price _____	Qty _____	Amount _____

> **Quantity Discount: 4 items→10%;**
> **7 items→15%; 10 items→20%**

Subtotal	_____
Discount	_____
Subtotal	_____
Sales Tax	_____
Shipping	_____
Total	_____

Sales Tax: Californians please add 7.5% sales tax

Shipping & Handling:
Book rate -- $3.50 for first book + $.75 each additional
Priority -- $4.50 for first book + $1.00 each additional

Name _____   Phone _____

Address _____

City State Zip _____

☐ Check enclosed $ _____   Date _____

☐ Charge my Visa/MC/Discover/AMEX $ _____

Credit card # _____   Exp. _____

Signature _____

Thank you!